Bicycle

in a

Ransacked

City:

An Elegy

Bicycle

in a

Ransacked

City:

An Elegy

BY ANDRÉS CERPA

Alice James Books
Farmington, Maine
www.alicejamesbooks.org

10 9 8 7 6 5 4 3 2 1

Alice James Books are published by Alice James Poetry Cooperative, Inc., an affiliate of the University of Maine at Farmington.

Alice James Books
114 Prescott Street
Farmington, ME 04938
www.alicejamesbooks.org

Names: Cerpa, Andrés, 1990- author.
Title: Bicycle in a ransacked city : an elegy / Andrés Cerpa.
Description: Farmington, ME : Alice James Books, [2019]
Identifiers: LCCN 2018020538 (print) | LCCN 2018021444 (ebook) | ISBN
   9781948579537 (eBook) | ISBN 9781938584978 (pbk. : alk. paper)
Classification: LCC PS3603.E747 (ebook) | LCC PS3603.E747 A6 2019 (print) |
   DDC 811/.6--dc23
LC record available at https://llcn.gov/201802538

Alice James Books gratefully acknowledges support from individual donors, private foundations, the University of Maine at Farmington, the National Endowment for the Arts, and the Amazon Literary Partnership.

Contents

Drift
For Tim—Newark, DE

Seasonal without Spring: Summer
So Close to an Ending
Buried in Darkness, Light

At the Tree Line

Orpheus in the Lost Amphitheater

Letter

If anything, I'm a petty thief in a world of forgetting, a blade in an elm,
a bottled note in the sea of Victory Boulevard at dusk.
Friends, family, gallows saints & ghosts, rig a swing at the edge of the shore
when I'm gone for the birds to perch & the bats to glide through,
to disappear & appear in the small places the moon cannot touch.
Thank you for the amorous & discontented beauty you saved for me here,
though most days, my silence was a soldier's slogged hand
hiding a match. I love you. I leave you the match.

Portrait & Shadow

The curtains sail into the room with the memory of presence behind them

while my father waits in the dark taking apart what is left of his former selves,
      like a pianist, drunk at the keys, playing the same four notes,

letting them ring in the pedals until they haul themselves back into sleep.

He says, *I am shadow*

& the thief at the seam of his spine slides through the blades of his shoulders,
      hollows the blood, while the dopamine cheapens

like a dollar-store lighter & suddenly, another streak in his Depends emerges as proof.

This too in Arcadia—

the meadow in twilight's last streak of red before he enters the tree line,

which is already waiting, its small footpaths like paintings held in storage,
      their deep palettes so close they strangle to a labyrinth

laced in an MRI-black. The wolf there tears at his tendons,

leaves him always in fog, & if he emerges it is only to watch but not to enter
　　　　the burning city & self he still loves.

He says, *I am the smoke's mascara*

& I know he is imagining the Bronx he can never return to,
　　　　where his youth is held in the thin frame of a bicycle

as it cuts through a billow of smoke. The city burned each night & each morning
　　　　he rose to ride through the rubble. The what was,

the father I hold onto in order to care for his shadow never gets old—

he is kind & clear, he rises each morning & lifts me onto the back of his bicycle,
　　　　he pedals while I glide above the city in wonder.

Freud Cycle—Untitled (Freud's Desk & Chair, Study Room 1938)

At breakfast I feed him my dreams as I arrange
his pills on the table. He is best in the morning,
when his wings lift from the labyrinth,
when he shaves, has an espresso.
Father, I dreamt last night that I was riding
a bicycle down a road in the country;
stones in my pockets to toss at the stray dogs.
I was afraid. The road continued into a fallen
green as the negligent moon took over the sky.
I could hear the dogs off in the distance
as I pedaled toward a clearing where one deer
stood; its proud antlers swayed in the silver
& I was silent. Silent as I've ever been. Calm.
Then you. You sprinted from the tree line:
openmouthed, unshaven, & took
the deer by its hind legs to drink your fill.
I wanted to run. I did. But ran toward you.

∞

Breakfast over: my father turns to his desk to shuffle his illegible papers in a three-card monte where no one wins. I stand at his back as if a cold wind stitched him a suit: child whose child is afraid. The wood of each locked drawer is varnish & depth, ash & shadow. I cannot open them. I cannot look into the chestnut & decipher the whorls. Easily, each day falls onto the desk & stains it while my father grows lighter. Soon, he'll be easy to carry. Soon, I'll walk into the room & he'll be almost translucent, calm. He'll have no need for the papers, the sound of the wind, or pills. In another decade, he'll have perfected the practice of absence. But for now, I ask for an answer.

He says, *In all likelihood you want to kill me*
but will only end up hurting yourself.

Wish fulfilled. I want him to say it again.
I want him to say the mad man
gets the milk; the squeaky wheel gets the oil;
that the dogs & the dead don't join us.

I want him to ask, why the stones?
or to rise from his desk & take one from his pocket.

To say, this is not protection,
it is a punishment like forgiveness.

Carry it when you go.

Notebook: The Kairos in Chronos

The way a slow day of drinking can unclutter the mind

    but clutter the room. Forget,

lilac dead on the desk as the cans compile. Then I went outside & stared at the same passage—

    four minds in a night-lit Berlin,

laughing, content with bringing their small rooms, patient study, each to each.

    Where are all the friends I could talk to?

When I began to love what is held in books more than the world,

    I was nourished. A door closed.

I walked a long hall & kissed the portrait of each friend nailed to the doors,

    the way in Barcelona,

one feather fell onto the blank of my notebook. The house we build is an imagined gallery.

The stanzas of their voices now distant,

distant, as a shackle of stars.

Tracing a Sparrow

The old truths are not written, they are not poems or held in bookshelves
  which fall & are buried like cities.

Instead, they continue the way a tattooed bird on a girl's back
  seems to rest, as if I, or no one, could open it,

shoot it down, or pull it from the life two fools
  imagined, incompletely & in earnest.

The inked sparrow in flight, lifelike, etched like a bleed of branches
  on the water at dawn.

And how well eternity is suited to youth, how all it wants to do is walk into itself
  with a thermos of wine & a bag full of crumbs for the birds.

When I was nineteen, I ate acid & watched the whorls in the floorboards fall
  beneath the varnish like a river into each gap between the planks.

I sat around & said the word *truth*. It was simple,
  the way I knew my lover would sleep through her first alarm,

then pull the curtains back & reach one hand into the world to check the weather,
  to feel the cold breeze & then place it

across my bare chest like the imprint of so many stars
  & their silence.

Gentle & hurried love before work. There was never enough time
  to coax the sparrow from its world,

so I spend my days at the library, visiting my dead friends
  who keep & refuse the same silence.

My lackluster training in the divine shows—I am no saint,
  I can barely live in this world without the chemical distortion of the other.

Two parts hell & one part heaven I've had. So tell eternity to do its worst,
  to stop dragging its hands along the chain link,

that I can see its reflection on the water, that a buried bird if you listen close
  will still sing. Among the yet to be

broken, are the lovers, the virgin drunks who have yet to sober or part,

& the woman who has not yet put the book down to stare at her life as if it will be another
  frail & fleeting thing she lost along the way.

Rosebud & the rest. Eternity with its one palm full of crumbs

for some common bird that lands & lifts with the same fear
  we must drown to live out our days, & its wings,

like a child's, whose fingers move along the etched spines of the stacks,

while his mother reads beneath the barred window next to me, leaving
  a crosswork of shadow on her right arm & shoulder

like the shadow she will keep until something light as a sparrow feeding,
  or one thought, wakes her into this life once more,

& her only choice will be to rise, to find her son who has not yet
  thought, *catacomb* or *knowledge*,

& walk with him the three blocks to the playground
  with eternity in her purse, waiting

to coax the sparrows from earth.

With a Fistful of Earth

How so soon after the funeral, there was laughter, & the children,
dressed in reverence, began to play, though they knew to hide some joy

while those closest to death waited for a moment that never came.

No eulogy is enough. No yellow lily on a chestnut coffin or fistful of earth.
No ritual. Nothing lasts, not even sorrow,

which is the iron clasp on the coffin that rings like a canary
after the singing. The bird brought into the light & the cage door open.

Tomorrow, it will be filled by the clean hands of morning,
so unlike the miner's soot-black hands

that lifted the yellow breast to his lips to say, *I'm sorry,
you weren't meant for this.* But like a childhood,

the cage door must close. The anarchy of smoke, the small fires

our ancestors kneeled toward to warm themselves, to stare into the distance
that had no border but the streaked gold that divided the land from sky.

Tomorrow. Black lace beneath a white linen shirt, the dream of death
which is hollowed in darkness. In working the thread of desire

the bodies become, for a slight moment, not separate, but dispersed.
The trees become silver when the snow descends,

& in that blur against the branches, a wolf steps into a buried trap,

yelps into the hourglass. But the leaf-light of late August comes.
The arthritic branches will gather sap. The children whittle them down

with the knives of their fathers & the patience of a woman, not yet showing,

looking into herself as the blue morning peers through a window.
At once, all things compile a palpable sense of presence & ruin.

Pine needles fall like rain, their scent's ascension in September's cathedral.

Seasonal without Spring: Autumn

When I woke for school the next day the sky was uniform & less than infinite
  with the confusion of autumn & my father

as he became distant with disease the way a boy falls beneath the ice,
  before the men that cannot save him—

the cold like a *forever* on his lips.

Soon, he was never up before us & we'd jump on the bed,
  wake up, wake up,

& my sister's hair was still in curls then, & my favorite photograph still hung:
  my father's back to us, leading a bicycle uphill.

At the top, the roads vanish & turn—

the leaves leant yellow in a frozen sprint of light, & there, the forward motion.

The nights I laid in the crutch of my parents' doorway & dreamt awake,
  listened like a field of snow,

I heard no answer. Then sleepless slept in my own arms beneath the window
  to the teacher's blank & lull—

Mrs. Belmont's lesson on Eden that year. Autumn: dusk:

my bicycle beside me in the withered & yet-to-be leaves,

& my eyes closed fast beneath the mystery of migration, the flock's rippled wake:

Notebook: The Kairos in Chronos

Rilke's language: Pleiad wings: the water

    & trams running through the deep October where I believed I didn't need any love.

What do you see or what do you dream?

    I see my life as a votive. My body a ditch. The great cities

a forest to loose in the burning.

    Nothing as wild as man. Boars coming down from the dark

& shot in the street. Green. Green. I miss you. I walked away with a notebook,

    five socks, my drugs, & two books.

Now I write *each night* in the morning.

    The moment before becomes an expanse. After, I find my face in the mirror.

A face like a room with one chair.

Fear of Intimacy

When my father tried to kill himself the first time, he ripped a telephone wire
from the wall of his hospital bedroom.

The next time it was a bedsheet. A nurse stopped him.

In his pockets were pencil notes: confessions for crimes he did not commit but felt
must have been the crimes of his punishment.

As the days continued the list grew like keloid scars from the DBS.

When I'd visit, he'd ask, *Was it in the papers?* When I'd leave he'd say, *Don't come back.*

His mind: the same sentences like a vinyl's skip the way they widened,
trailed & returned.

As he kissed my mother in the ward's cafeteria he whispered, *I am Judas.*

When my father's mind became the small wheel in my chest, I didn't want to love anyone
I didn't already love & those I loved I hid from.

I broke up with my girlfriend. Smoked outside Beth Israel & took the long way home.

At the end of each avenue, everyone who was left I watched as if they were
on the horizon & could break

at any moment. Then what?

I'd have to wade in, find the fragments & clear my already empty studio,
wake to the shadow of something half-finished & continue—

the currency of love is self-sacrifice.

Pilgrimage

How often I've leafed down Broadway, my face half hidden

& found the night to be another failed suture—

seven miles of heel touching heel, scar cleaning scar,

as the wind frisks my hands for crumbs. I have loved this city

in ways imaginable, learned not to speak when speaking,

to scry its palms. Yet too soon the gulls slit

the borrowed night into a thin blue ether: the blank pages

of a journal forgotten—the middle chapter,

our ghosts. I was safe as a quelled dream in the dark.

Notebook: The Kairos in Chronos

Either I'm in a windowless room with one mirror, or singing "The Thrill is Gone"

    with a fistful of synapse

on mute. After a decade of bars, rooftops, & corners

    so much of life is wake, rush

& no high.

    The conductor steps out at the last station in snow.

And the sanitation boys,

    with Styrofoam cups in their hands, truck in first gear,

    wait on that *good city pension*

& a radio call. Like a coat left on a barstool—

    I am watching,

because watching's what's left.

Despair & Fire

I dreamt my veins were lit like the Seine, but the walls in front of me
held only half-constructed bridges of rip & fog, over a fading lily
wallpaper where so often the flash of sirens marred by the barred windows
became a wilderness before our eyes. For your birthday,
you wanted to shoot up in Strawberry Fields & I couldn't say no—
us so innocent in our will not to live & if we danced then
it was because the room was empty & without music like a boy's fist.
You hoped, that past twilight, the fireflies would emerge
like a distant city you could eventually rise to touch.
But it was summer & the day lasted too long to watch them begin.
Instead, you sat silent at the window as children
flipped from the fire escape onto a mattress, their Chuck Taylors scuffed
like burnt hydrangeas, or the sound of one now-sober daughter
coming home. Tarot & filth & the Cyrillic script of the fires
that were almost spectacular, the way they tossed themselves into the streets,
while below them, whole families had no choice but to pray,
knowing they were banished & already forgotten like the needle
you tossed from the window: oar for the pavement,
after joining hands with a neighbor's child, the future
thin & outside the body, something more than permanent.
Once, on a rooftop, *How much do you love me? & what would you do if I jumped?*

Notebook: The Kairos in Chronos

Failure & its association with disease. The sadness of it all. Choices

so many choices become the day. A child pretending to be sick for attention.

Me, blackout drunk, as she drives me home—

Do you love me, do you love me, am I interesting or romantic & why?

A voice that could theoretically solve it all.

A word. Like bullshit talk about the weather,

I spent the day in a dissociated whirl. My computer's been open for an hour now

& all these words are just some interior system I've built to survive. Bad idea.

So much synapse & Ian's photograph of three birds with translucent skin,

just beginning,

openmouthed, ignored in the chaos, starved.

Seasonal without Spring: Winter

Despair, & the page open to the forest of Dante's suicides
        while a blue bird cocks its head on the sill

framed by an obliterate sky. All last night the Glock's *Oh lord*
        at attention

poised as a starved wolf in snow.

The brown tap filling my glass this morning, & my dehydrated heart's
        sprint—more & more aware of my blood,

that songbird's natural & frail precision

like Billie's beautiful haunt. The ghost enters the city, (*Gregorio*)
        a nicotine streak in his beard

& his body: one violin warped in the black

tire-eaten snow. *In hell*, he says, *a woodpecker like a harpy*
        eats at my heart.

Yesterday, I spoke to the branches leant by the first snow.
        I was angry & jealous of their belief in spring.

The world requires unrequited patience—

the statue of a woman holding a tome, sparrow
   shit on her frozen shoulders.

When I snapped a few branches, the green in each mocked me:
   Look at you, pathetic, bent to winter

& *frail.* Behind my door there is no need to greet the world.
   Maybe I won't leave today.

I say this to no one,

my breath white as the sparse walls, or a marble mattress,
   as I bathe in cold water

then think again of the forest in hell, its amplified terror,

knowing Dante's death mask wears a frown, as if hell
   were worse than he imagined.

Without Sleep

Botched silence like the dual blooms of riot police zip ties, or a spliff lit
on the back of a Harley. In the pitch,

I open my knife like a flashlight over the water. A figure in the distance,
a flutter in my eye—

nothing's there, or Nothing's there.

In the darkest-before, dust dies early in the atmosphere & the lovers come out,
find the least polluted dark,

hoping to see traces in the night like the play of light on a web.
The stars hung themselves. In the moment between

the floor's disappearance & the snap of the neck—constellation.

If god is dead I mourn him by rubbing dirt into the whorls of my hands. Snapped branch
& fate. She quoted her favorite novel, *It's all so strange, such sorrow*

& then pancakes after... The remnants' pilot-blue flare. Dust in the corners,
       mold on the dishes, ash on the lip of a can. By not sleeping,

the conifers last like sharks.

⸻⧓⸻

A leopard with its one paw outside the chain-link corner of its cage, *If only,*
       if only...
Hunger. Cart coffee & donuts, the boils on the crossing guard's left wrist:
       a biography written in snow, or

flaw becomes prayer.

⸻⧓⸻

Ripples like snakes at high tide. Rain like threads in a loom. Maybe birth is a séance,
       or the habit of never staying too long.

Feral ribs in bramble: completion that says I know I'll live forever knowing I'll die.
       At the spine of the water, a gun tucked under my belt,

I watch the twilight's dance of two pitts in a black mirror: one roan, one blue.

Lauren—Vondelpark, Amsterdam

The photo of this lover is already sepia & static, burnt at one edge.

Her pupils: two windows in a darkened room.

◁▷

Tonight, the fog says, *You are whole*, but the body differs

      & no self-portrait will tell you otherwise
      & no wide landscape will accept you, broken as you are.

I outlived the moment I thought I should die, next to her,

      on a clear day, where we watched white cranes
      lift from the dark waters;

the world willing to accept us, whole, just this once—

      and I said no.

The Distance between Love & My Language

She, no one, can hold my blood like a trembling mirror in which the stars can weep,

& therefore, I walk the city unknown. I'd like to vow my silence & be done.
I can't. I keep a belief in salvation,

in a hand reaching gently out. The click of dice in lamplight, a chewed cigar,
& my friends raising guns to the air on a rooftop,

painting the sky with their anger. The wolves' communion, my death,

my box of ashes in a pause of wind. I don't wanna be holy,
I want my breath to flock & spiral like birds,

but like a girl, so far from the ocean, whistling a hollow-point into the wheat fields

at twilight, as she watches her song carry, I think, *Where does it end?*

Powerless in love, I dreamt the deep shade of Berlin; that distance was my savior,
yet I still wanted to hold the birdcage & dwindling song: my father's chest,

& hold my mother's strength, to be there when she weeps. I wanted another life,

one in which my love could save them. Years after our love had ended, in its first form,
an old lover asked if I could speak, if I could finally let a woman in,

& then I remembered how she began to shatter plates as her hands trembled, when I had no words but a bottle's silence or shatter. We broke

everything that night, & cared deeply at the end. We thought about their beauty,
about the waste, the money we'd have to spend.

The language of our anger was frail.

It was the cheap nourishment of forgetting, not the hand, the thumb moving in a slight circular
motion to ease & say, *I'm ready*.

There is a language I can't take back, a rib cage cleaned by the wolves & scattered,
a tint of red in a snow which lays my love distant. I remember taking my father's throat

in my left hand, while my right hesitated, made snow of the Sheetrock beside him.

At the Water

Mud; the early frescos I left in a lean-to, in the slats & the wine dark by the shore.

They wait in the distance with the rest of my sleep, as the tugboats pass
through an industrial blur.

I am again watching this place, from a dull green Civic, waiting to enter.

Then the radio goes dim. The car door goes mute. The oil-slick night takes its rag to my jaw.

Where I drew god's answer to Job, a woman, balanced on the tracks of the Staten Island Railway,
fifty years shut down sometime in my youth, is flooding tonight.

Behind her, an open window, gull-white razors & the last child throwing bread
into the light as the birds follow.

In the distance, the tracks continue, rusting over the water while the slats drift out.

I come to this shore, a frame on the abyss, because it feels like myself: tired & trying
to move from halogen to a shimmer on the water.

This gets old & I get older, stubborn, but the place becomes a friend.

How could it not when this world is so often the bulletproof box at the deli revolving, the moment when the figure behind the glass becomes opaque & it seems as though nothing has entered.

Three Sheets to the Wind

Home isn't too far past the Blue & Gray on Castleton
        Avenue, where a guitarist plays
all night for his drinks. I stop in

& motion, *One more*, until Despair
        is hauled out by the bouncer.
In the parking lot, he's hot-blooded & drunk

in the wings, running his mouth like always,
        tire iron in hand:
How old was your pop when he got sick.

 Answer: *44. So that means you're past halfway,*
        & more than halfway
to being nothing. Last Saturday, same time,

same place: *Fuck it, you should try*
        & kill yourself too.
He knows where I live & he's on his way,

so I cut through the park. From the top of the hill
        I can see my apartment & the ill-lit
windmills across the water in the west.

The cracked lettering of my thrift store jacket
        says *Field*. It keeps me halfway warm,

so all I can ask for now is one Newport

& a bagged beer. I don't want to go home,
          I keep walking the darkest-
before-dawn. Briefly, the shadow of trees

on the wall & their reflection, among mine,
          in the deli window: a latent, gnarled
forest in a field: Cain's dog whistle & pocketknife.

While I'm out here buying my time,
          Despair's in the wings with a spare key,
in the stairwell, decorating my apartment

with a cutout of my favorite word in her last letter:
          Yours, my father's loon-bin self-portrait,
& a still life titled, *Apple & Gun*.

Notebook: The Kairos in Chronos

Outside the Village Vanguard I watched myself punch through the window of a taxi & walk away.

The surprise in that music. Rye in the ice.

Newness in the hull of history.

But if the horn section dismantled & walked quietly into the bathroom to smoke,

to ash in a dehydrated yellow,

there would still be the stage.

"Man is religious by nature,"

but I was purposefully irreverent, & therefore became immaculate & reverent,

as the carefully rolled spliffs that prepared us for the moments we hoped to collect—

the gossamer of each day hidden by traffic.

I was angry, disappointed by life, & happy. I was just 18.

Rome

The light followed her hand, touched the dark table, the cards laid out like ash,
solitary, clear, & the sweat on the brows of the years in the air, giving it texture.

Doesn't a life turn, or at least begin like this?

When suddenly a woman breaks through the surface of her marriage, her daily routine,
which, though they were young, was too soon laced in a failure

they could not name. She decided to leave: *just a week*, not the vow of *until*,
but a week. She kissed him at the airport

& said she'd call—his voice was distant that first night

as she laid, jet-lagged, in a set of stark linens, the window slightly open,
& the sun coming down. The sage in the vase was sweet.

She walked, without a camera, through the once grand lobby & into a sketch
of another life: lamplight against the ruins, carafes with cheap wine,

Caravaggios, & teens making calls to their dealers, separate from the crowd,
as the last pigeons bathed in dust. It was not the Spanish Steps,

or the Trevi Fountain. It was the lives that were not hers,
it was Rome's ancient lust

surrounding the holy city, how a walk like that could make one pure again.

At the Sistine Chapel she sat & looked up. The last time she said *god*
they were in bed & how strange it is to say *god* when one doesn't believe.

She said to herself, *I'm not supposed to think this here, the pope would not approve,*
& then returned to that scene: her husband beneath her

& her saying *god*, her hand on his chest slipping finger by finger away.
Maybe she was his god & he not hers,

or maybe she was closer to begetting him…the womb etc.

She planned to return & sketched the scene:

she would have to explain, at least a little, what the week meant to her,
she would make love to him as a sign. He would want her,

he would want to know she still wanted him, but she would not say *god*

in their love, because god is simply a veil that says, *mortal.*
She would say *mortal* instead.

The Theory of the Flat World

Falling, the way sleep descends & lingers in the dulled yet emerging folds
        unfolding. Clarity & static like the psych ward lounge's

bang-it-till-it-works TV. My father drooling before it when I entered,
        & as I left, lost in the Plexiglas, he spun in a slow shuffle,

in a thin, pale-green issued, unshaven, ass out & let me mention it again, lost. Four months
        without sunlight & every day I visited. Yet I wanted to choose

my own life. My body over his. Not my body for his.

If I leave he won't remember me. If I leave he won't remember he was young once,
        he'll have no mirror with which to look back.

He'll try to kill himself again. He'll try to kill himself again…

⊸⧓⊸

Barcelona. Among my friends, I burnt a cigarette into my wrist like a botched tattoo—
        I'll sleep when I'm dead.

Then I watched the ember flood from the skin as the filter pressed to a numb,
        loved how the pain was almost not there,

how it twined in the rooftop's lace. Everyone was what they were:
        primal in a flickering numb.

Then each drink cut with rainwater.

The crowd in the stairwell when I turned my wrist, let it branch
        from the edge

to let the rain enter the wound. Not to cleanse,
        but to deepen.

I detested the body, but loved the world so:

⬯⬯⬯

        the joy of my own destruction: the molecular spirit broken down.

Scarred, I bathed in the plazas until dawn, my shirt open, hoping to catch
        the faintest breeze on my chest. Lost lover.

Fool's gold. Father & a wreath of dead wings. When I pressed my ear to the earth there,
        the traffic sounded like home.

The shell of my ear always sounded like home.

Morning Journal

she washed my hands with rosewater: empty cathedral:
beach town in winter: snaps above the smoke rings
as the hearts unfurl: last week's flowers hung
on a doorknob: drying: brittle: the sparks of their petals
on wormwood: in the mirror slow as motes in a window
she said *I can't stay*: the thumbprint of her voice
from somewhere deep in the morning's green-gray sea:
brush fire: breeze in the pines: her bare steps
in a doorway: sand in the linen: sand in my palms:

At the Castle of Sant Ferran

The war is over. And as if no one had ever died
the swallows keep turning from the windows into god's silence

while in this century, blind, forgotten, nooned into submission,
into shadow like a ghost laid into the mortar

I barter with them: bury me, the blades of my shoulders
in the blue altar & I'll come clean.

I'll drink from that well. I'll leave.
To the deer: let me go unnoticed,

let me watch as you take from the earth the seed of your stone.
I'll give everything back. Light as a brushstroke

I'll veer into the 21st century: to the noosed skid marks
& laughter. That life. That city, catacomb, steel & glass

for bone. Mine. All that I am heir to: hubcaps, carbon,
cardboard & pavement; my father's body

his crown of fog. Before I must claim that
impermanence, if it is any different from these hours,

I would like to walk the broken stones once more
here, alone with the ghosts & the silent living,

freed, as death frees us from history, within history
& in near silent ruin.

Notebook: The Kairos in Chronos

After a night of self sabotage, a determination to obliterate the day,

I woke in a thin sheet, later than I was supposed to,

to the sound of the already birds. In summer,

I love to join them that way,

like walking into a bar where your friends have saved you a seat.

Colin with his backpack on, standing to greet me.

Julia's laugh as I kiss the back of her neck.

If only I could enact the common wisdom.

The strong money tree, I sometimes forget to water, trembles with the blinds in a breeze.

I've grown so fond of it, the tree.

When I wake & there are no birds, or Julia's gone,

it is here, in this studio apartment,

in one of the three windows that open to nothing special: a wall.

The Lesson

I say goodnight, smile, walk out the door then sit on the hill
        above, & facing my father's house, smoke another
spliff & watch his, then my mother's, windows go dim.

I believe that maybe in the streetlight which flickers & reflects
        off the stop sign, at the plateaued road between us,
a flutter, a baseball card in a wheel, will conjure a former self

to slip from my old window, to walk here & sit with me awhile,
        with his shoulder to my shoulder
as he takes a few drags, sighs then says, *I'm going back home.*

I wouldn't say things gets better. I'd say, *We learn to live,*
        that, *human beings can get used to anything.*
But he already knows this somewhere, though he'll have to

throw bottles off rooftops, piss himself & sleep in the snow,
        wake to his corruptible body & shame,
withdraw, close one hand around his father's throat

like a nail you'd hang a mirror on, as the right hand hammers
        the Sheetrock & his mother tries to calm him,
crying, blaming herself & holding her palms to her son's cheeks

as he steps back, wipes his eyes until the Sheetrock damps
        against his veins. He'll have to walk
alone for years to thaw the ash & numb.

Bronx Nekyia

I felt as though the ghosts had left us, that the trash & insulation strewn across the floor
        were the cave paintings of addicts so lonely & dead

their only art became to trace the fate of all cities, as they gradually become grand,
        empty & unknown. It seemed I had no choice

but to wait until the room reached outside of itself to pull in the dark,
        like a sailor pulls a net from the sea,

the edge of the boat a tangible threshold, while the other threshold, the horizon
        becomes one with the sky,

a wall the ghosts peer through like a child holding one eye to the bullet hole
        in the elevator door—black ripples in a wall of steel.

Long tired of the cackled laughter, I now know why they close the eyes of the dead
        & why, unknowingly, in some secret ritual, my mother kissed each eye

        before I left—*Our boy, our beautiful baby boy.*

There is a point when no guardian can explain the world, & language reaches its end,
        though nothing ends, & the child rides beyond the pitched horizon,

like a ship in the theory of an infinite fall.

Notebook: The Kairos in Chronos

Deep inside the benzos he falls asleep beneath a summer rain & wakes with the smell of it

in his fist like a cortex. Is it leaving this world clean

that matters? Admit it,

yes you, he & me, Mr. Cerpa, that you & most of your friends are apathetic & joyfully sad

& that's why you've gathered & gather at every windowless I-don't-give-a-shit in this world.

And why everywhere you go you walk aimless & away

& don't double back, but hail cabs so far from your bed that those deep leather seats feel like a bed.

Every cafe table & ruin of Barcelona

cast in a votive light, like remembering Lauren as she leant back & looked away.

Her smoke. A few strands on the bedside table.

The place I frequent around here has an oak bar wide enough to put your head into, among the grain of other desireless men. *So it goes* or *here we go again*—

summer rain, pollen,

    fecund on my white Nikes, gray hoodie, & jeans.

Drift

Beyond the street, bramble, an abandoned dock, then the water.
      As I cross, my friends trod forward

& descend. Traffic at my back, a furrow of foliage forgotten, tangled
      with human rejection—trash bags, beer cans, twine, etc.

Before we reach the dock, which opens to oil tankers & industrial New Jersey,

my friends' footsteps are the only light. At the water, the makeshift stars
      break free. The question of what to offer

the body—an echo in the cave's hum. Wild for wild's sake. Synthetic ritual.
      My body the invisible night,

a rush of piss joining the water from above. Leant back with my back
      to the guards & guardians, the streets where sirens pass.

Then Jenny brings the fecund storm to her lips, & notices, in the water,
      what must be lost—neon lilies: jellyfish,

silent & amorphous, led by what laps the sun-dyed driftwood onto black sand.
      The pull of wonder, & finally, I weep again for joy.

For Tim — Newark, DE

Somewhere in summer my friends are burning through cane and cold beers in a 'twas heaven prayer card.

Between now and there I don't say much more than, *How's the weather?* to the rain.

It turns to snow.

Winter is the knife I carry but never use & we're dying but dying slow & that's life.

You scared?

I'm no longer sure my friends can save me.

But once I dreamt that death was a struggle for the last words you don't find, then you wake & everyone's there playing whiffle ball again.

In the house we shared there was static & the trains shook the windows as they left.

I want to shake like that again.

The grass is always greener & the dead think so too, but they learn to let go.

I haven't.

My jacket's been stitched in dear lord & late birdsong; in black branches & ice.

And my youth, I hold it, like a stove top holds a blue flame, or how a child holds a revolver: guilty, thrilled in a black corner of the attic.

This is the brutal joy of moving closer to sleep.

Your head on the bar while we dance.

I'm walking through snow now, banished, not saying much & hoping I can become like you: stripped of every decadence: light as the light on the floorboards.

Notebook: The Kairos in Chronos

To walk alone in the city, to live without night, I stayed high for a decade

& believed it was love.

Write me a letter I won't answer. Please.

But that time is over. And the leaves on the chess tables of Washington Square Park

are lit & precise as I cross. Dinners at her apartment.

The movies at IFC. The sex & the laughter

& the terrible thought of losing it all.

Spalding Gray— *"Maybe I should try to live as though the world was going to go on forever."*

What moment or moments compiled to this thought?

& what changes when one is led by a sentence into a different unknown?

Like any other Sunday, Julia & I woke together, made love, & then fell back asleep.

In the calm I saw it—all aimless, worthwhile, & slow.

Seasonal without Spring: Summer

I dozed on the handball court in the noon's non-shadow until it was hard to see anything
        but the splotched sun—

a cut in the reel,

        then the spliced imagination on screen between the actual scenes of my life
        held in a locked room, all through summer.

Was that season artery or vein?

        When the days stretched like Broadway,
        & the nights undid our shirts—

the temperature so slight you could raise your arms in flight & feel nothing,
        the body as air.

But there was also the need for hurt.

And dusk: a ghost of a boy tempted to feel his weight, to put his palm to the depth,
        touch the pupil, the dead turbine
        of god's one good cataracted eye.

And the clouds throwing shadows on the reservoir until it was the color of Jason's gun—
        glean & black.

Sweat stains & thirst. The year of my first fight
        & the pavement on my cheek like depression—

Devon at my back screaming, *Get the fuck up*. Blood on a leaf, one woman with child
        at the shore, & the barges at our part of the Narrows
        came back empty & singing

the way a dead tree creaks in the wind, sways in unison
        among the rest.

A dream is the web without the spider,

        the soft snap of rot—still so real to me, in a pristine ruin
        like her shower & the fogged glass

where we split a Pabst in the morning, before work, hungover, & trying to hold off
        the day. The light doesn't hit my windows until noon now,

& quick as a razor across a stale Phillie, memory flares with autumn's black leaves:
        vanished cane-break: the pillars at the memorial

in Berlin, where I walked & she emerged & was gone in a peripheral & measured
        descent—a minnow sky

& children with their elbows braced like a hen waiting to be clutched,
        played there. Hid.

        The city muffled their voices. The memorial muffles Berlin.

At a café table—*even the dead are dying.*

But the sky above my childhood home, edging down the hill, is a painting I carry, cast
      in a cheap gold frame, to every room I've lived in since.

I came to art when I found myself in a dark wood, early in life,

because those years are like a house already sold, the furniture gone
      & the new picture frames not yet nailed to the walls—

what remains: there were lives in those rooms & there are lives there no more,
      like this summer, when I drove past

the summers spent drinking in a Little League diamond, John in the distance
      waving his phone to make trail marks in the outfield,

& Mike, next to me on the guitar, whose voice is still in the air there,
      the way sometimes I believe

I've always been asleep on a long ride home.

Let the earth do what it will—

      have me, spin the spokes until my memory fades to a ruthless spring.

So Close to an Ending

We were drinking because we knew it was over & couldn't change,
didn't want to—

always not yet & the last time I saw her, white breath in the darkness,
when she raised her arms then dropped to her knees saying, *I can't take it anymore,*

how many times can the same thing happen?
Earlier, she wanted to bring a stray into the car & I wanted to go home,

said, *Nothing you save will save you,* or *let nature take it course.*

Most days, I want to lay down in the dark architecture like the buried half of a wheel,
but sometimes I can't & can't figure out why, like my father holding

the incontinent dog he refuses to put down, & carries, though each day streams of yellow
fall on the rug. Something about the sun drenched in my window,

wolf song in the tree line, the horizon & other locations
where the two worlds collide like two bodies in a deep bright

hidden, make me want to hold on. When she rose she pushed her hair back
& a few strands calved forward. I stepped back. It was over.

We locked eyes & drove home.

One last time under the vaulted ceilings, & as we dressed in a quiet mirror,
each of our backs held the red braids of each other's fingers, claw marks

& longing, the memory of what little comfort we could give: the scars of old wings.

Buried in Darkness, Light

A tree fallen in the ferns turning a bright termite brown at its center,
or the spider of tar closing over my lungs. In light of decay,

the light of decay breathes through its yellow teeth, clear as birdsong,
begging, *Ether, come home*. All the night's loose follicles

lean latent in their breaking like harp strings, dope fiends,
or a songbird's illegible heart. Asleep on the train riding nowhere, I laid my head

into the rain-stained copies of the AM paper, my repeating dreams
under the surface in heroin's grip. There are psych ward songs

of comfort somewhere behind the brick, butterfly knives tearing names
at the shatterproof glass where the gone lips of a lover lingered in fog,

& though the facades are silent as birch bark, something deep in the steel
sings, the cells rupture against the still-drawn curtains

the way a mind folds its sparks like a child told too often to *Pipe down*.
Above the station, a man weeps as he lunges toward the hem of each coat,

the bone beneath his right shin exposed, clean against the dull neon clatter
& flesh. In the early years, Mike & I walked a trail of pine needles

& blunt guts through Central Park, pretending to embrace decay,
to disappear but never leave

like a subway car turning a corner, its light not yet reaching the rails ahead.

Notebook: The Kairos in Chronos

Lost & certain or certainly lost I walk outside on a Friday thinking, *No matter who it hurts,*

    I'm gonna drink myself back into ether.

One powerful intimate moment after the next—

    a note written in vain,

her back & my arms in the troubled-water reflection of a black TV,

    then both of us bare, so light, so gentle & geometrically sure.

In a poem by René Char I read, *"transparent storms"*

    & looked for their equivalent in life.

Rain enclosing the earth, or the way I switch from good man to degenerate fast?

    Beyond dusk & the sun's slow performance, Julia calls.

And though I've developed a new kind of drinking,

    that I believe is a punishment for her acceptance & love,

I'm trying to learn a few things

& appreciate this sky coded in language,

the days that become me,

that whittle me down.

At the Tree Line

That year I rented a room without mirrors & smoked dope with my friends, alone, every chance I could get. The morning of my 22nd birthday, Bill pushed a bundle through the gap in my door & put two shots in our morning coffee. I went to work, read, got off early. Even though the house was empty there was always a palpable sense of return—slant-soled shoes on the floorboards, whorls & piles of ash, a book laid open to its spine. Already dark, I watched a movie & called my father. His voice like thin smoke in blue light—

⁀⁀

In art there is comfort, control & revision.
Iñárritu's *Biutiful* for example, where the son dies
& is met by his father, younger than him,

who offers safe passage & advice, a cigarette:
one last earthy comfort. In the tree line—fog, the sound
of the father's footsteps, the promise of the sea.

More likely, my father dies surrounded by the sterile
beep of suicidal green, tendered by the touch of a stranger
who will go home & outlive us both.

More likely, we are not met at the end. There are no words
or safe passage. Yet I, like you, can say whatever it is
I'd like to say about death. It is a vacant city

filling with birds. My father will meet me there.
The sins of this earth will be forgiven.
Maybe, death is too old to become tragic,

it's had its fun, has already slipped down oblivion's
staircase & lays there, broken, looking up,
as the new gods saddle up & turn the hourglass over.

I will begin again, in my father's car—
the September he sat us down & told us
he would not die, but change.
The September when I asked
the simple questions of childhood

plainly, he said, *This is what it does to you*,
the brakes clenched at a red light
outside of school, *look*:

tremors: so many birds rising in unison
& without reason, mazed
in the rearview mirror, gone.

There is a current beneath us, a river
frozen as hell mimicking first the bare
branches, then sky. Whatever fear I choose,
the mirror, the shack of the mind
singed to the skyline or drowning,
a thread like the broken stars
keeps hauling me back.

Tonight, I do not want to tell you my name
to hear it repeated. I want to scrape
my one chair to the middle of the room
& smoke alone with my burnt-to-shit coffee.
Maybe by morning I can walk outside

& watch my father's car glide to a stop.
Say, *Not today Dad.*
I don't want to go means I want to go with you.

Notebook: The Kairos in Chronos

At the Guggenheim, on Sunday, early, my father & I are walking,

    entering rooms as he begins to slow & fog.

The Parkinson's like birth & death in each season. Each season in a day. He cracks jokes,

    stares, & I hold his shoulder,

consciously trying to touch, reaffirm, & comfort.

    This is what passes for happiness. Is happiness now.

Well, we walk & keep walking.

    I think, *Wind does not preclude light.*

But now that I'm twenty-six, which sounds foolish, I know, dear reader,

    I am learning, unlearning,

as Picasso's *Woman Ironing,* in that blue after, put all her skeletal weight into neating just one thing.

I miss you already was the song of my youth.

It was a slow, good morning here,

here in this world, my one life, next to my father's.

Orpheus in the Lost Amphitheater

When I emerged, it was dusk & I learned that this too is hell,
an afterlife, the center of a lost amphitheater whose seats
are a deep moss, wet-black with yesterday's rain. As I faced west,
the sun, obscured by the pines, shone in the gaps, pulsed
as it mimicked her descent: the heart beneath her delicate ribs
that I've lost each day anew. It was then, in that first dusk,
that all the abstract longing of the world, twined from her sinew,
became song: her eyes: April: the frame with which the gods had placed
a great silence, that stirred & released the need for sight,
when she came—blushed & final. Even the field that had her
without me on our wedding day. I imagine that too.
It is not true that I moved the great stones. I only built chords
from the restless pull of untouched bodies in the barracks
of dreams. In the half circle of the ear, she returns to me,
like the few strange bats dispersed in that first dusk, their clicks,
their songs that flare with all that is imperceptible & kind.
My song returns the shape of her frame. I walked in hell, & walk
in hell among the living. I turned back. Therefore,
I have learned the world's secret: that all is lost, even the losing.

HERIBERTO CERPA, PhD.
August 12th 1956 - March 5th 2017

Acknowledgments

Mom, your love & generosity live in me each day. Thank you. You are our rock & our joy.
All the light in this book results from the light you & Dad created together.
I will love you always.

Ileana, my sister, we were there together. You give me life & hope in the face of despair.
Thank you for your love & all of the laughter.

Jeanne Murray Walker, my first poetry teacher, you saw me. I am eternally grateful for your
guidance & trust.

Colin Schmidt, without your brilliance I'd be lost. You are my brother in poetry & this one life.

Michael Curley Jr., thank you for the hours & the music. It was beautiful.

Much love to everyone on Center St.—especially, Daniel Levine, Ryan "Telly" Shea, Ian Platz,
Ryan Conaty, Ben Morrison, Matthew Paparone & Billy Bartz.

Many thanks to my teachers, the homies & the great fires.

The generous support of the MacDowell Colony & the Rutgers University-Newark MFA program
nourished me during the creation of this book.

My warm thanks to the editors & staffs of the following publications in which these poems first appeared (sometimes in earlier versions) for their generous support of this work.

"Freud Cycle — Untitled (Freud's Desk & Chair, Study Room, 1938)" —*Hayden's Ferry Review*

"Fear of Intimacy" — *Bellevue Literary Review*

"Seasonal without Spring: Autumn" — The Academy of American Poets Poem-a-Day

"Seasonal without Spring: Winter" & "Portrait & Shadow" — *Kenyon Review*

"Buried in Darkness, Light" — *West Branch*

"Notebook" portions of this manuscript were published by *Devil's Lake, West Branch, & Horsethief*

"For Tim — Newark, DE" — *RHINO*

"At the Tree Line" — *RHINO* — selected as the 2017 Editor's Choice Award

"Bronx Nekyia" — *Perigee*

"At the Castle of San Ferran" — *Radar Poetry*

"Orpheus in the Lost Ampitheater" — *Triquarterly*

"Seasonal without Spring: Summer" — *Gulf Coast*

"Without Sleep" — *Third Coast*

"At the Water" — *Glass: A Journal of Poetry*

"Despair & Fire" & "Without Sleep" were featured on Episode 3 of *POETA* — 8 Ball TV, directed by Andrew Basilia.

Recent Titles from Alice James Books

Alice James Books has been publishing poetry since 1973. The press was founded in Boston, Massachusetts as a cooperative wherein authors performed the day-to-day undertakings of the press. This collaborative element remains viable even today, as authors who publish with the press are also invited to become members of the editorial board and participate in editorial decisions at the press. The editorial board selects manuscripts for publication via the press's annual, national competition, the Alice James Award. AJB remains committed to its founders' original mission to support women poets, while expanding upon the scope to include poets of all genders, backgrounds, and stages of their careers. In keeping with our efforts to foster equity and inclusivity in publishing and the literary arts, AJB seeks out poets whose writing possesses the range, depth, and ability to cultivate empathy in our world and to dynamically push against silence. The press was named for Alice James, sister to William and Henry, whose extraordinary gift for writing went unrecognized during her lifetime.

DESIGNED BY

PAMELA A. CONSOLAZIO

Spark design

· Printed by McNaughton & Gunn